D1497830

PRAYER

"The prayers of all saints upon the Golden Altar which was before the throne."

—Revelation 8:3

"Where the Golden Altar fumed."

—*Paradise Lost*, XI:20

PRAYER
At the Golden Altar

by

Clarence Edward Macartney

Minister, First Presbyterian Church, Pittsburgh, Pa.

ZONDERVAN PUBLISHING HOUSE
Grand Rapids, Michigan

EIGHT FORTY-SEVEN OTTAWA AVE.
GRAND RAPIDS, MICHIGAN

FOREWORD

The events of the second World War, as might have been expected, have brought the subject of prayer to the front in a new and impressive manner. The newspapers report the prayers of men going into battle, floating on rubber rafts on the sea, or fighting the enemy in battles above the clouds. At home millions of parents, children, husbands and wives, brothers and sisters are praying for their loved ones who are waging bitter and bloody battles. But war or no war, prayer is an ever timely subject.

In these sermons I have avoided a discussion of the so-called theological and philosophical problems of prayer, such as the reconciliation of the determination and predestination by God of all events and the influencing of those events by our prayers. In such discussions, however interesting they may be from a purely intellectual standpoint, there is little profit for the soul. In these sermons, preached on Sunday nights to men and women in the midst of life's battles and perils and temptations, I have tried to illustrate and demonstrate the power of prayer, and to encourage them so that, as Jesus said, they might always *pray, and not . . . faint.*

CLARENCE EDWARD MACARTNEY

Pittsburgh, Pa.

CONTENTS

CONTENTS

I
PRAYER'S DELIVERANCE

Seek the Lord and his strength
(I Chron. 16:11)

I

PRAYER'S DELIVERANCE

Seek the Lord and his strength (I Chron. 16:11).

The world was stirred by the story of the rescue of Captain Rickenbacker and his seven companions from death after weeks of drifting in rubber rafts in the vast waters of the Pacific. Not the least moving part of that deliverance was the story of how these men, some of them unbelievers and scoffers, in their distress turned to God in prayer. One of them had a Service New Testament, and Rickenbacker and this man took turns reading from the Testament at their nightly prayer meetings. After many days of drifting, when they were near death from starvation, they decided to pray audibly — although no doubt most of them had already been doing so silently — to God for deliverance.

Not long after this prayer meeting, a sea gull, searching the vast deep for its food, saw the rubber raft and lighted on Captain Rickenbacker's head. While the others held their breath, slowly and cautiously Rickenbacker raised his right arm, knowing that death or life depended upon whether he caught the gull or not. Suddenly he seized the bird in his hand, quickly tore it to pieces and divided it among his starving mates. The flesh of the sea gull saved him and his companions from death. Rickenbacker himself frankly attributed the deliverance to a divine intervention. A more striking testimony, however, was that of his pilot, Whittaker. Whittaker confessed that he had been an atheist and a scoffer, but when, after the prayer meeting, the sea gull had been captured, and when superhuman strength had been given him and his two companions to paddle their raft against a strong current and reach safety on a coral island, he changed, so he declared, from an agnostic and an atheist to a firm believer, to one who desired to acknowledge God and show gratitude to Him for His mercies. He had made,

11

he said, the greatest of all discoveries: he had discovered God.

Like beacons of light in the darkness of this present tragic war which is raging throughout the world, are the testimonies of men in the air, on the land and on the sea, to the power of prayer. In the foxholes of Bataan there were no atheists. An American pilot, flying over the Mediterranean to bomb an Italian port, tells us that his bombardier was reading his Bible until the very moment of action. Barney Ross, the former prizefighter, writes that in a pit in Guadalcanal he and three wounded mates prayed for an hour during a Japanese bombing attack. The gripping book *Three Men on a Raft* relates that three airmen, after five days in their four-by-eight rubber raft, at the suggestion of one of the men, a lad from Missouri, prayed. That night it rained, and they were delivered from death. From all the fighting fronts these encouraging testimonies are coming to us at home.

I. MAN IS INCURABLY RELIGIOUS

These testimonies which show how men in the time of great distress, facing death, turn to God in earnest prayer, reveal that man at heart is uncurably religious and that he has an unbreakable relationship with God. The shock of imminent death may be required to awaken some men to the fact that they have souls, that they have to do with God; but so it has been from the beginning. Psalm 107 contains a vivid description of a storm at sea, and tells us that the sailors, when they were desperate and the ship was about to sink, cried to the Lord in their trouble. *They that go down to the sea in ships, that do business in great waters; these see the works of the Lord, and his wonders in the deep.* Adversity and trial reveal the religious nature of man.

There are those who are inclined to ridicule the prayers of Rickenbacker and his companions and the three men on the raft, and say that they were of little value; that fear made these men turn to God. Fear of death is a great reality, and that reality made these men aware of that greater reality, which is God. The test, of course, is: *Will these men keep on praying?* There was once a godless seaman who was fishing with his companions, and a storm arose which threatened to sink the ship. His companions begged him to offer a prayer; but he demurred, saying that for years he had not prayed nor entered a church. Finally, upon their insistence, he made this prayer: "O Lord, I have not asked You for anything for fifteen years, and if You deliver us out of this storm and bring us safely to land again, I promise that I will not bother You again for another fifteen years!" There is no doubt that many of those who pray earnestly in the time of great distress, afterward, when the storm is over and the danger is past, forget God; but that in no way invalidates the fact that in their distress and danger they realized that there was a Power higher than themselves, and that they turned to that Power in earnest supplication.

II. THE FOUNDATION ON WHICH PRAYER STANDS

After I had read that moving narrative of how Rickenbacker and his men in their hour of danger turned to God in prayer, and when I read that their deliverance convinced them that God is, and that He hears prayer, I asked myself, as perhaps you did: *What would have happened if that sea gull had not lighted on Rickenbacker's head? If the rain had not fallen that night after the three men in the raft had prayed for rain, would they have died without faith in God and regarded prayer as a vain delusion?* The point that I wish to make is this: our confidence and belief in prayer must not rest upon what to us is a manifest and indisputable answer to prayer. Perhaps beyond the horizon there on the vast Pacific there were other airmen who had come down on the sea, floating about in their rubber raft, anxiously scanning the heavens for the sight of a rescuing plane and the horizon for the masts or stacks of a vessel, who prayed just as earnestly as Rickenbacker and his companions or those three men on the raft for deliverance; but no deliverance had come. The long days in the glaring sun had been succeeded by weary nights; the sharks had circled about them, and at length they had perished of hunger, thirst and exposure. What about their prayers? Shall we say that prayer is a reality only for some people, only for those who get the answer for which they are asking? Thus we see that our confidence in prayer must not rest upon a particular answer. It must rest upon the fact of God, His nature and His love, as revealed to us in the Scriptures; upon the example of the prophets, the apostles and Jesus Himself in the practice of prayer; upon the invincible instinct of the heart, which in the time of man's weakness and helplessness makes him turn to God and ask for the Rock that is higher than he.

There are answers beyond our answers, that is, beyond what seem to us to be answers. David lay on the ground all night and prayed for the recovery of that child of love and sin; but the prayer, as he asked it, was not answered. The child died; but David did not cease to pray and to believe in prayer. He comforted himself and said of the child, *I shall go to him, but he shall not return to me*. Paul prayed earnestly. He besought the Lord three times that his grievous and painful thorn in the flesh might be taken from him, but his prayer, in that form, was not granted. The thorn remained to buffet him and harass him to the end of his days. Yet at the same time God answered him when he prayed, and this was His answer: *My grace is sufficient for thee*. Paul found that to be true.

Spiritual and moral calamity would result if one's faith in God and faith in prayer depended upon answers about which there is no doubt in one's mind. "But," one asks, "did Christ not say to His disciples, and to us, *If ye ask any thing in my*

*name, I will do it . . . Ask, and it shall be given you . . .
knock, and it shall be opened unto you . . . Whatsoever you
shall ask in prayer, believing, ye shall receive"?* Yes, but we
have mentioned two godly men who asked, believing, and
what they asked was not granted them. One of them, Paul,
asked it in the Name of Christ. When Jesus says that anything we ask of God in His Name will be given us, there is
implicit, of course, in such a promise those limitations which
Jesus Himself recognized in His own prayer, for, in His
great prayer in Gethsemane, in His hour of anguish, when
He sweat the bloody sweat and prayed, *If it be possible, let
this cup pass from me,* He added what you and I must always
add to our prayers: *Nevertheless not my will, but thine, be
done.* That is the one prayer which you can make and always
be sure that it will be answered: *Thy will be done.* John
gives us the same promise which Jesus gave regarding answered prayer, but makes *explicit* the limitation which is
implicit in the words of Jesus. John says, *And this is the
confidence that we have in him, that, if we ask any thing
according to his will, he heareth us.*

III. THE BENEFITS OF PRAYER

The benefits of prayer are many. One is this: prayer
brings you into fellowship and communion with God your
Maker. When Alexander Stephens, Vice-President of the
Confederate States, was a prisoner at Fort Warren, after the
fall of the Confederacy, he wrote in his diary the following
description of the dull routine of the prisoner's day: "He
undresses and stretches himself on his bunk. Here with
soul devout he endeavors through prayer to commune with
God. To the Eternal, in weakness and full consciousness of
his own frailty, the prisoner commits himself, saying from
the heart, 'Thy will, and not mine, be done.'" Harold Dick-
son, one of the three men who for thirty-four days drifted
a thousand miles in a four-by-eight rubber raft, with no food

and no water, said of the prayer meetings which they held each night: "There was a comfort in passing our burden to Someone bigger than we in this empty vastness. Further, the common devotion drew us together, since it seemed we no longer depended entirely upon each other, but could appeal simultaneously to a Fourth that we three held equally in reverence."

The men's reference to a "Fourth" with them in the raft reminds one of those three Hebrew lads in the fiery furnace, who prayed to God and put their trust in God. When Nebuchadnezzar came to look into the fiery furnace to see what had happened to them, he saw that they were unharmed by the flames, and, lo, in the midst of them, he saw the form of a Fourth, like the Son of God. That is one of the great blessings of prayer. It gives you fellowship with the Fourth, with God, with Jesus Christ, the Saviour of men. The Psalmist said, *The Lord is nigh unto all them that call upon him, to all that call upon him in truth.* Earnest prayer brings you near to God and makes you aware of the fact that God is always near to you.

Again, prayer shows us the difference between right and wrong and arms us for the battle with sin. Prayer strips the disguise from the face of temptation. Milton, in *Paradise Lost*, represents Satan as coming first in the guise of a toad to spy out man's garden and plot for his overthrow. But wise Ithuriel, the archangel, touched the toad with the point of his spear, and, lo, Satan in all his malignancy stood upright. Thus prayer reveals to you the presence and the temptation of Satan.

Prayer is your greatest help in the midst of temptation. It is the sharpest weapon that you can wield. When you have failed to pray, and have been overcome, then it is prayer — and only prayer — that will help you find your way back to God.

IV. ENCOURAGEMENT IN PRAYER

The Bible encourages us in prayer. We are inspired by the example of men who prayed — patriarchs, prophets, apostles, martyrs and, above all, the supreme, sublime example, the Lord Jesus Christ Himself. We are encouraged to pray for everything that pertains to our lives. In the Bible we read of men who prayed for everything. Hannah prayed for children. Solomon prayed for wisdom to reign and rule over the people. Paul prayed for freedom to preach the Gospel. David prayed for forgiveness. The dying thief prayed for a place in heaven. Pray for anything that you desire, but always with submission to God, and with the prayer that His will may be done.

CONCLUSION

Try prayer. When you are angry and inclined to "strike back," try prayer. When you are disappointed in your work and prospects, or in those whom you love, try prayer. When you are in doubt or perplexed as to the way to take, try prayer. When you are anxious and burdened, try prayer. Cast all your care upon God. *Cast thy burden upon the Lord, and he shall sustain thee.* When you are tempted to do evil, try prayer. When you have been wounded by the darts of Satan, try prayer. Never despair. Never faint, but always pray.

II
PRAYER AND THE SOUL'S RESERVES

The people that do know their God shall
be strong, and do exploits (Dan. 11:32)

PRAYER AND THE SOUL'S RESERVES

The people that do know their God shall be strong, and do exploits (Dan. 11:32).

Before and at the beginning of this war Germany rang with such slogans as "Strength Through Joy" and "Strength Through Youth." Today the slogan is "Strength Through Grief"; but the Christian slogan is "Strength Through Prayer." *The people that do know their God shall be strong, and do exploits.* Prayer helps men to know God.

The Bible has much to say about strength. If you look in a concordance you will find that there are few words which occur more frequently in the Bible than the words "strong," "strength" and "strengthen." The first inference, therefore, is this: we need strength on our journey through life. We need strength against ourselves, against sorrow and temptation and sin and death. Great is the soul's need for strength. The second inference from the Bible's constant use of these words "strength" and "strong" is this: our souls are capable of great strength. That constant exhortation to be strong would not ring through the Bible from beginning to end as it does unless we were capable of exerting and using great strength.

God did not have time to make a nobody. When He created man in His image, He created a being with great capacity. There are three proofs of man's greatness: the first is his creation in the image of God; the second, the price that was paid for his redemption when Christ died on the Cross; and the third, man's capacity to be strong, to be brave, to endure, to overcome. In Psalm 103 the Psalmist says, *Bless the Lord, O my soul: and all that is within me, bless his holy name.* All that is within you — who can measure that?

What words can describe it? In the parable of the talents Christ taught that although men may differ in their gifts and endowments, all men have talent and ability. If we are called to great tasks and great achievements in life, a great capacity is lodged in us. Men sometimes speak about the pathos of uninvested talents and powers, about genius which has never had an opportunity to show its power. That was what Gray had in mind when he wrote his beautiful lines about the venerable graves in the Country Church Yard at Stoke-Poges:

> Perhaps in this neglected spot is laid
> Some heart once pregnant with celestial fire;
> Hands that the rod of empire might have swayed,
> Or waked to ecstasy the living lyre.

If there is a pathos and a mystery in these hidden powers of life which do not assert themselves, there is also, it seems to me, a deeper pathos in the fact that in the battle of life men are often weak when they might be strong because they do not avail themselves of the power that is lodged within them. That is a power which is awakened by prayer. We arm ourselves by prayer with strength. *The people that do know their God shall be strong, and do exploits.* Picture a great modern cannon. The long and graceful barrel of the gun points toward the foe, but there is no power in that barrel. A wheel elevates and lowers the gun, but there is nothing in that wheel itself which can repulse the enemy. The range finder is a delicate and beautiful instrument, but it is powerless in itself. The shell, or cartridge, is ready to be hurled against the foe, but there is nothing in that shell by itself which can injure the enemy. Behind the gun is the gunner ready to do his work with a strong mind and a trained hand, but in him there is no power that can harm the enemy. Only when the spark of fire is applied to the powder can the great cannon with its intricate mechanism, death-dealing shell and trained gunner become an instrument of power and destruction. Similarly, prayer is **the** spark that brings the powers of man into action.

I. PRAYER AND ADVERSITY

In the hour of adversity they who know their God in prayer shall be strong. There are many men who overcame physical adversity and handicap and "took captivity captive." John Milton, whose light was spent "ere half my days, in this dark world and wide," courageously sailed the sea of trouble and in spite of his blindness made mankind his debtor forever. John Calvin, who was seldom well, yet toiled nobly for humanity, left to his heirs a fortune in furniture and stocks and bonds of two hundred dollars, but to the world he gave a purer Reformation, republican liberty and the kindred spirit of republican institutions. Above all others towers Paul with his thorn in the flesh. Most men would have retired from life's activities, but not Paul. He prayed earnestly about this thorn and asked that it might be removed. The thorn was not taken from him, but divine strength was granted him to accomplish his almost incredible achievements. Those thousand-mile journeys over mountain and desert, those dangerous and stormy voyages through the Aegean and the Mediterranean demanded great strength and endurance. Prayer gives one courage to bear the burden of physical infirmity, and, as we have seen, will supply an energy which makes possible great things in spite of physical difficulties.

Another form of adversity is sorrow and affliction. The waves of sorrow sometimes sweep over the soul and threaten to put out the lamp of its hope and its courage. On the morning on which Abraham Lincoln buried his son Willie — an affliction which bowed him to the ground with sorrow and almost incapacitated him for his public duties—Lincoln went into his chamber, and said to a friend, "I will try to go to God with my sorrow." Take your sorrow to God. He asks you to cast the burden of it upon Him. *Surely he hath borne our griefs, and carried our sorrows.* How many I see who are overcome by their sorrow and incapacitated for life's duties through paralyzing and crippling grief. But in your sorrow there is always the possibility of endurance, of conquest and of victory through the power of prayer. Through prayer in the time of sorrow you can know your God and be strong.

II. PRAYER AND TEMPTATION

Temptation is a universal experience. It is also a dangerous experience, for within all of us there is that which responds to the solicitation of temptation. There are temptations to fear, to doubt, to cowardice, to unbelief, to injustice, to cruelty, to hatred, to despair, to impurity. But remember that there is no temptation which is too strong for a praying soul. Prayer discovers the temptation and arms the soul in advance against it. King Arthur won his great victories with the sword "Excalibur," which came out of the mysterious deep and which, when he had fought his last battle, he returned to the deep. That is a parable of life and of prayer. There is a sword bathed in heaven — a sword which comes out of the unseen that we can use in the battle of life. In the old hymn we sing, "Temptations lose their power when Thou art nigh," and it is prayer that makes Christ nigh to our souls. In his anchorite's cave in the desert, St. Anthony, tempted by voluptuous women and wicked demons and satyrs, was about to fall, when suddenly a light shone in his cave and he saw the face of Christ, and was strong.

Temptation is always to be feared, for it is always dangerous, but by prayer it can be overcome. *Watch ye and pray*, said Christ, *lest ye enter into temptation*, which means: "Pray, lest temptation overtake you and overcome you." When Admiral Farragut asked Admiral Dupont why he had failed in the attempt to take his ships into Charleston Harbor, Dupont gave a number of reasons for that failure. After listening to them, Farragut said, "The real reason for your failure, Dupont, was that you did not believe that you could do it." Temptation is powerful; but he who believes that he has the power to resist it and overcome it in Christ always wins the victory, and, strong in the strength which God supplies, treads all the powers of darkness down.

III. PRAYER IN THE TIME OF DEFEAT AND SIN

The time of defeat and sin is the most critical hour. Everything depends upon what the soul will do in that crisis. It may seem that exhortations, prayers, aspirations and good habits have been in vain. They apparently were not able to bind the strong man of evil within the soul. Is it going to give up the war because one battle has been lost? Is it going to surrender to evil? Is it going to accept the subtle lie of Satan that there can be no repentance and no recovery? Will the soul again enter the battle? How stirring are the accounts of those men who were wounded and overcome by temptation and sin, but who, girding themselves with prayer, rose out of the dust and conquered their grim foe. In spite of his spiritual nature, his holy aspirations, his beautiful Psalms, his devotion to God's honor, David fell and sinned terribly, and Satan must have rejoiced in the confidence that he now had David in his power. But that was not the end of the battle. David prayed and called upon God. He confessed his sin: *Have mercy upon me, O God . . . blot out my transgressions. Against thee, thee only, have I sinned, and done this evil in thy sight . . . Wash me, and I shall be whiter than snow . . . Create in me a clean heart, O God; and renew a right spirit within me. Cast me not away from thy presence; and take not thy holy spirit from me. Restore unto me the joy of thy salvation; and uphold me with thy free spirit. Then will I teach transgressors thy ways; and sinners shall be converted unto thee.*

That prayer is being answered! David, by his example, his repentance and his prayer, is teaching transgressors God's ways; perhaps he is sounding the trumpet of hope for some reader who has sinned against God and against his own soul.

Who was more terribly defeated by Satan in the battle of temptation than Peter? Who can describe the bitterness, remorse, self-loathing and shame of Peter when he went out that night from the courtyard of Caiaphas where he had denied his Lord and wept bitterly? How grimly significant are the words: . . . *and wept bitterly.* We know that those bitter tears were the tears of prayer. Each tear was a prayer, each prayer a tear. Let us read the Acts. Who was that preacher who on the Day of Pentecost stood before the scribes, the Pharisees and the murderers of Christ and told them that with wicked hands they had slain the Prince of Glory? Who was that brave soul who, ordered to desist from preaching or be cast into prison, declared that he would obey God rather than man? Who wrote letters to the persecuted disciples of Jesus, telling them to count it joy and glory when they were called upon to suffer for His sake? It was that same Peter who went out into the night and wept bitterly, but who would not accept that defeat as final, and called upon God out of the depths. God heard him and delivered him!

In his great allegory, Bunyan tells us that in the battle with Apollyon, Christian, hard-pressed by his grim foe, the Black Fiend, fell to the ground and his sword slipped from his hand. The Prince of Darkness lifted his weapon to dispatch him, but at that moment Christian closed his hand once again on the hilt of his sword, and leaping to his feet, cried out, "Rejoice not against me, O my enemy; when I fall I will arise again!" With that he drove the Black Fiend from the field. Yes, great are the powers of recovery. Great are the reserves of every soul, when prayer calls them into action.

By prayer men are made strong. *The people that do know their God shall be strong, and do exploits.* Paul has a great passage in which he calls upon the believer to be strong in the Lord and in the power of His might; and then, referring to the various parts of the Roman armor of that day, he tells the troubled and tempted man how to arm himself: to put on the whole armor of God, the helmet of salvation, the breastplate of righteousness, the shield of faith and the sword of the Spirit. Finally, he exhorts us *to pray always with all prayer and supplication in the Spirit, and watching thereunto with all perseverance.* In other words, those pieces of armor and those weapons of offense and defense are of no use unless they are brought into action by prayer. Prayer puts the armor on! Prayer fights the battle!

> From strength to strength go on;
> Wrestle and fight and pray.
> Tread all the powers of darkness down,
> And win the well fought day.

III

YOUR UNANSWERED PRAYERS

For this thing I besought the Lord thrice,
that it might depart from me (II Cor. 12:8)

YOUR UNANSWERED PRAYERS

For this thing I besought the Lord thrice, that it might depart
from me (II Cor. 12:8).

One evening after I had preached a sermon on prayer, a woman greeted me and reminded me that she had been praying for the recovery of a sick sister and had asked me to join her in her prayers. "Now," she said, "God has answered our prayers." At once I said, "I am glad to hear that. It will be a joy to you to know that your sister's life is to be spared." "No," she replied, "my sister is dying. She cannot live."

This woman had prayed for her sister's recovery, but her sister was dying. Nevertheless, she was sure that God would answer her prayer. God always hears and answers a worthy and sincere prayer. But ofttimes the answer is "No." Those who have never heard God's "No" have not prayed frequently.

There is no subject which is of deeper interest to man than the subject of prayer. Yet men are often puzzled by two facts which they cannot reconcile. They know the promises concerning prayer and feel the wonder of the fact that the Almighty God should answer the prayer of a human soul, yet at the same time, they are oppressed by the thought of God's omnipotence and the laws which He has established for His universe. "Can it be," they ask, "that Omnipotence would turn aside from the usual course of events to hear and answer the prayer of a mortal being?" But the desire to pray is always present. Prayer is the spontaneous act of the soul in the time of distress or deep desire. Like the man in Christ's parable who went to his neighbor's door and knocked on it, man, in the midnight of the soul, calls upon his Eternal Friend.

I. WHEN PRAYERS ARE NOT ANSWERED

We have the great promise of Christ that if we ask anything in His Name, it will be granted us. Yet, often when we prayed earnestly and in the Name of Christ, what we requested was not granted us. The answer was "No." Why some prayers are not answered we do not know. "The things that are revealed belong unto us and unto our children. The things which are hid belong unto God." God may say "No" to our prayers and give no reason why our petitions were not answered. We trust Him for His grace. He has His own good reason. Christ once said, *In that day ye shall ask me nothing.* In that future day of complete revelation we shall not need to ask why our prayers were not answered, for then all things will be made clear and we will see that the answer "No" was for our good, the good of others and to the glory of God.

> God hath His mysteries of grace —
> Ways that we cannot tell;
> He hides them deep, like the hidden sleep
> Of him He loved so well.*

The Bible declares that God will not answer the prayer that issues from an insincere or evil heart. When we say this, we do not mean that a man who is out of Christ, or who is the victim of an evil habit, should not pray for deliverance; but insincerity of purpose in coming to God and the retention of evil in one's life will make prayer ineffectual. Peter tells men to treat their wives with kindness, *that your prayers be not hindered.* The Psalmist says, *If I regard iniquity in my heart, the Lord will not hear me.* Our Saviour warns that an unrelenting, unforgiving heart will hinder our prayers. A man may pray for the highest good in the Christian life, and yet, if his heart is full of hatred for a brother, or if he refuses to forgive someone who has offended him, his prayer will not be heard. Jesus said, *When ye stand*

---

* From "The Burial of Moses," by C. F. Alexander.

praying, forgive, if ye have aught against any . . . But if ye do not forgive, neither will your Father which is in heaven forgive your trespasses. He also tells us that before we come to worship and to pray we must be reconciled to our brother who is alienated from us.

What seems to be no answer on the part of God, or what seems to be a refusal of our prayer, may, in the end, prove to be a delayed answer. In the two parables on prayer which Christ gave us to encourage us in our prayers — the parable of the man who knocked at midnight on his neighbor's door, until, to be rid of the annoyance, the man arose and granted his request, and the parable of the unjust judge who finally granted the widow's request to avenge her of her adversary, so that he might be free from her importunity and continual coming — Jesus taught not only that we are to persevere in our prayers and be earnest in them, but also that the answer may be long in coming. Mary and Martha sent the message to Jesus, *He whom thou lovest is sick,* supposing that the Lord would come at once. But He remained where He was three days, and when at last He started, Lazarus was dead. When He reached Bethany, Martha said to Him, *Lord, if thou hadst been here, my brother had not died,* as if to reproach Him gently for not having come to them at once. But that delay was to be to the glory of God, and resulted in the conversion of men to Christ and the comfort of these sisters. Restoring Lazarus to them, raising him from the dead, was of far greater importance than healing him of his sickness before he was dead.

The story of the raising of the daughter of Jairus tells of a similar delay. When Jesus heard the request of the ruler of the synagogue at Capernaum to come and heal his little daughter, He started at once, but on the way, the woman with the issue of blood touched the hem of His garment as He passed down the street, and Jesus stopped and spoke with her. When He was ready to start again, a messenger came to Jairus, saying, *Thy daughter is dead: why troublest thou the Master any further?* While Christ tarried the child died. But Jesus said to Jairus, *Be not afraid, only believe.* Presently Jairus found out what that command meant, for Jesus restored the damsel to life. I used to hear my father in his prayers quote these words spoken by Paul: *Now unto him that is able to do exceeding abundantly above all that we ask or think.* How often that has been proved to be true! What seemed God's "No" in the beginning eventually proved to be a far more glorious answer than we had expected.

II. GREAT EXAMPLES OF UNANSWERED PRAYER

We cannot ignore the fact that there are many unanswered prayers, that is, in the sense that what was asked for was not granted. If by some angelic power I could search the heart of everyone who reads this book and repeat to you all the prayers that have been asked but have not been answered, what a collection it would be: unanswered prayers for the coming of a child; for the life of a little child who was sick; for the recovery of a loved friend; for the conversion of a soul; for the securing of a position; for some success or happiness in life; for deliverance from some peril. But these requests have not been granted. God in His wisdom has not seen fit to give what was asked. But if you have uttered prayers which have not been answered, you can have the assurance that you are in high and distinguished company. If you have asked God for something and His answer has been "No," you are in the company of men like Samuel, who prayed for another chance for Saul; like Moses, who besought God to let him cross the Jordan into the Promised Land; like David, who asked God to heal his little child; like Paul, who thrice besought the Lord to take the thorn out of his flesh; like our Lord Himself, who prayed in Gethsemane's shadows that the cup might pass from Him.

THE PRAYER OF MOSES

Out of the Bible's many examples of the unanswered prayers of godly men, I shall select two, that of Moses, the greatest man in the Old Testament, and that of Paul, the greatest man in the New Testament.

On the way out of Egypt to the Promised Land, the people murmured at Rephidim because they had no water, and said, *Would God that we had died when our brethren died before the Lord! . . . Why have ye brought up the congregation of the Lord into this wilderness, that we and our cattle should die there?* Greatly troubled, Moses and Aaron fell on their faces before the Lord at the door of the Tabernacle. Then God spoke to Moses and told him to take the rod, the wonder-working rod, and speak to the rock before the people. Moses assembled the people before the rock, and cried out to them, *Hear now, ye rebels, must we fetch you water out of this rock?* He lifted his hand and smote the rock twice, and abundant streams of water flowed forth.

There was something improper in the conduct of Moses. Just what it was that offended God we do not know. Therefore, God said to him, and to Aaron also, *Because ye believed me not, to sanctify me in the eyes of the children of Israel, therefore, ye shall not bring this congregation into the land which I have given them.*

Soon after this, Aaron and his son, Eleazar, were conducted to the top of Mt. Hor. There Moses divested Aaron of his priestly garments and put them on Eleazar, his son. But Aaron died on the mount. Moses' punishment was not long in coming. When he had finished his great work for Israel and had led the oft-rebelling and oft-complaining people as far as the River Jordan, he had to give way to another leader, Joshua. Because of his past offense — the smiting of the rock — he was not permitted to cross over into the Promised Land. What a great disappointment that must have been to Moses! We can understand how he must have felt when he was removed from his great position when he was so near the goal. He was permitted to stand on Pisgah's summit and "view the landscape o'er"; but he was not allowed to cross the Jordan into that Promised Land. No wonder Moses prayed and besought the Lord, saying, *O Lord God, thou hast begun to show thy servant thy greatness, and thy mighty hand . . . I pray thee, let me go over, and see the good land that is beyond Jordan, that goodly mountain, and Lebanon.* But the Lord answered Moses, *Speak no more unto me of this matter. Get thee up into the top of Pisgah, and lift up thine eyes westward, and northward, and southward, and eastward, and behold it with thine eyes: for thou shalt not go over this Jordan.*

God's answer to Moses' earnest prayer was "No." Yet Moses had the comfort of God's words and of God's presence. God did not forsake him in the wilderness, although He refused to answer his prayer. There on Nebo's lonely mountain God buried His servant. But that was not the end of the history. In a certain sense, Moses waited for three thousand years before his prayer was answered. You cannot read the story of Moses' prayer and God's "No" when He buried him in Beth-peor without remembering what happened centuries after on a mount which was perhaps visible that day to the eyes of Moses when he looked longingly from Pisgah's summit over the Promised Land. Moses had desired to see God's glory in the conquest of the land beyond the Jordan. Long ages after he had prayed that he might enter the Promised Land, he was raised from his lonely mountain grave and with Elijah beheld the glory of the Lord and spoke with Christ concerning His decease which He should accomplish at Jerusalem, that is, the great work of redemption, of which Moses himself was a prophet and of which the deliverance of Israel out of Egypt was a type. God's final answers are greater than those for which we ask.

By Nebo's lonely mountain,
　On this side Jordan's wave,
In a vale in the land of Moab,
　There lies a lonely grave.
And no man dug that sepulcher,
　And no man saw it e'er;
For the angels of God upturned the sod,
　And laid the dead man there.

In that deep grave without a name,
　Whence his uncoffined clay
Shall break again — most wondrous thought! —
　Before the Judgment Day,
And stand with glory wrapt around
　On the hills he never trod,
And speak of the strife that won our life
　Through Christ, the incarnate God.

O lonely grave in Moab's land!
　O dark Beth-peor's hill!
Speak to these curious hearts of ours,
　And teach them to be still.*

PAUL'S UNANSWERED PRAYER

After I had prayed with a man who had been bedridden for many months with a painful affliction, he said to me: "Yes; this morning the pain was terrible, and I said, 'Father, if You are willing, take away this pain.' But He didn't do it. The pain grew worse." I told him I did not know why God did not answer his prayer. Then I told him of Paul's prayer that the thorn might be plucked out of his flesh, and that his prayer was not answered, but God said unto him, *My grace is sufficient for thee.* Paul's experience may help many praying souls to hold on to God, and show them that through patience and the comfort of the Scriptures they may have hope.

After his beatific vision, when he had been caught up into the third heaven and heard and saw such things as it was not lawful for man to utter, Paul was afflicted with what he called a *thorn in the flesh.* It was something very grievous and painful, so that he called it a *messenger of*

* From "The Burial of Moses," by C. F. Alexander.

Satan to buffet me. What it was we do not know. Some think that Paul was speaking figuratively, and that by his *thorn in the flesh* he meant some distress of mind or spirit, such as remorse over his past persecution of Christ and His disciples or the enmity and persecution of his enemies. Possibly it was a temptation of the flesh. That would not be strange, for some of the greatest spiritual leaders, such as St. Jerome, Augustine and Anthony have experienced such temptations. If the *thorn in the flesh* referred to such temptations, we can see why Paul described it as a *messenger of Satan*. We can understand, too, why he spoke of the civil war within his breast, the law of sin and the law of the mind, and why he said that he strove always to keep the body under, lest *when I have preached to others, I myself should be a castaway*.

However, it seems more probable that Paul's thorn in the flesh was a literal affliction of his body. Some have thought that it was malarial fever. Perhaps that was the reason why, when he landed at Perga, on the southern shore of Asia Minor, which was in a low, malarial region, Paul did not tarry there but went at once to the highlands of Galatia. That coincides with what he said to the Galatians in his letters, namely, that through an infirmity of the flesh he had preached the Gospel to them.

Others think that Paul's thorn in the flesh was a disease of the eyes, then a common affliction in the Near East, and distressingly prevalent today. Such an affliction could be described as a thorn, or stake, thrust into his flesh. *My temptation which was in my flesh*, Paul said, *ye despised not, nor rejected . . . I bear you record, that, if it had been possible, ye would have plucked out your own eyes, and have given them to me*. This and other passages, it seems to me, support the theory that Paul's thorn in the flesh was a disease of the eyes.

Whatever the painful affliction was, Paul prayed out of

his distress in great earnestness, and *thrice*, which does not mean that he prayed three times, but over and over again, that the thorn might be taken from him. But the request was not granted. Instead, Christ said to him, *My grace is sufficient for thee: for my strength is made perfect in weakness.* The answer, you see, was not the granting of Paul's request that the thorn might be taken from him, but the gift of strength to bear it and endure it. So great was this gift that, in spite of his affliction, Paul was able to accomplish wonders, even physical wonders, in his work for Christ, and could say, *Most gladly therefore will I rather glory in my infirmities, that the power of Christ may rest upon me.* It was for Paul's good and for the world's good and for our spiritual instruction that Paul's prayer was not answered. This is true of every earnest prayer, answered or unanswered. Every prayer strengthens the soul with the presence of God. Our Lord Himself experienced this. When He prayed to have the cup pass from Him, the answer was "No," but an angel from heaven came to strengthen Him. We can always be assured of heavenly strength and comfort.

> If called like Abram's child to climb
>   The hill of sacrifice,
> Some angel may be there in time,
>   Deliverance shall arise.
>
> Or if some darker lot be good,
>   O teach us to endure
> The sorrow, pain or solitude
>   That makes the spirit pure.

I like to imagine what we shall think and feel and see when we get to heaven and all things are made clear, when we see no longer through a glass darkly, but face to face. One thing, I believe, will be this: we shall see how wise and kind God was in not answering some of the prayers which we addressed to Him, for, if we had obtained that for which we asked, it would not have been for the welfare of our souls. I am sure, also, that in heaven we shall understand how many of our seemingly unanswered prayers which were for things in accordance with God's will and, as far as we could tell, were for our good, were answered in a way far beyond our thoughts and dreams. Then we shall know the glorious truth of the statement that God is able to do far above all that we can ask or think.

IV
YOUR HINDERED PRAYERS

That your prayers be not hindered

(I Peter 3:7)

IV

YOUR HINDERED PRAYERS

That your prayers be not hindered (I Peter 3:7).

Few persons, I suppose, have read the sequel to Robinson Crusoe's story of his captivity on the lonely island. In this sequel he tells how he revisited the island and endeavored to convert to Christianity the mixed colony of Englishmen and natives. Most notorious among these islanders was the wicked and profligate seaman, Will Atkins. When it was suggested to Atkins that he and his companions teach their wives religion, he responded, "How should we teach them religion? Should we talk to them of God and Jesus Christ, and heaven and hell, it would make them laugh at us." Defoe relates Atkins' efforts to tell his wife about God, and describes his difficulties and eventual success.

Although the hindrance was overcome through sincere repentance, the difficulty which Atkins encountered in praying with and for his wife is an excellent illustration of what the apostle means when he says that men are to honor and love their wives, that their prayers be not hindered. Because of his own past conduct the sailor found it difficult to talk with his wife about God and to pray for her.

Hindered prayer — what is it? It is the prayer that pulls itself down and defeats itself when uttered, or which is not uttered at all. There is a mystery and a problem about our unanswered prayers. Why the fervent prayer of a good man, uttered in the Name of Christ for a worthy object, such as removal from temptation or the conversion of a soul, should not be answered and the petition granted, we cannot tell. Not until we stand beside the Golden Altar itself shall we know. But there are unanswered prayers about which there is no mystery. Whether the prayer was hindered in its utterance and never asked, or whether, having been asked, it was

43

unanswered, the reason for it is in the man who prays. *Ye ask,* says James, *and receive not, because ye ask amiss.*

Peter, in this passage we are considering, is giving advice — and good advice — to husbands and wives. Easily and naturally he descends from a grand utterance about the atonement of Christ to household and domestic duties. What he has to say is in strange contrast with the revolting popular literature of today which deals with the relationship of husbands and wives. Peter tells wives to respect and obey their husbands, with the hope that by their Christian conduct they may be the means of converting them. In conversation they are to be chaste; in dress, modest. Today all distinction between pagan and Christian dress has been lost. The ornament of a meek and quiet spirit Peter commends to these women, as being in the sight of God of great price. There is no earthly relationship capable of such high happiness and blessedness as the marriage union. But it is also true that there is no relationship in which sin produces such misery as in marriage. To the husbands, who, to a degree, have the happiness of their wives in their keeping, the apostle makes his appeal to deal with their wives considerately and to honor them, *that your prayers be not hindered.* He does not mean that self-control and mutual respect in this relationship will cause their prayers to be answered, but that dishonor, disrespect and unkindness in such a relationship will hinder their prayers.

Peter's counsel recognizes that life and all its duties must be regarded in connection with the highest duty and relationship: our duty to God and our life with Him. We are to judge everything in this world — every labor, every amusement, every friendship — by that standard.

I. AN EVIL CONSCIENCE KEEPS MEN FROM PRAYING

Unworthy living, of which the abuse of one's wife is an example, rises up to confront a man when he comes to the

Golden Altar of prayer. There are two ways in which sin hinders a man's prayers. In the first place, it may hinder him from praying at all. His evil conscience condemns him and keeps him from praying just at the time when he needs prayer most. The man who has been abusing his wife is in no mood to pray; and what is true of that sin is true of others. He feels unworthy and inconsistent when he prays. It may be, too, that even the desire for prayer is destroyed by his conduct. Sin separates man from God; it dims the desire to know God. This is a self-evident truth and stands by its own arithmetic. The man who hates is not likely to pray for the spirit of love and forgiveness; the sensualist is not likely to pray for purity; the lying man is not likely to pray for honest and truth-speaking lips. Such a man feels out of place at the altar of prayer. I do not mean, of course, that men who are subject to these temptations, or scarred with the sins which result from yielding to them, cannot pray and have no desire to pray. Certainly, when the spirit of repentance moves them, they can and will pray, and God will answer them. I mean this: these and other sins, indulged in and neither repented of nor renounced with resolution, hinder a man's prayers, and either confuse him when he comes to pray or silence altogether the voice of his petition. The reason which some men give for not attending church is not always the reason which they mention, whatever that excuse may be; the real reason is often this: when they do go, sin hinders them and makes them feel unhappy and out of place.

The Rime of the Ancient Mariner presents the poetic conception of how sin hinders prayer. After the ancient mariner had killed the sacred albatross, in his distress he tried to pray. But his lips could not pronounce the words:

> I looked to heaven, and tried to pray;
> But or ever a prayer had gusht,
> A wicked whisper came, and made
> My heart as dry as dust.

Only after his repentance and the spell of judgment had been lifted was he able to pray and set out on his pilgrimage from land to land, to teach by his own example love and reverence to all things that God made and loves. The great poem concludes with the ancient mariner's declaration of his delight in going to church to pray with the goodly company:

> To walk together to the kirk,
> And all together pray,
> While each to his great Father bends,
> Old men, and babes, and loving friends
> And youths and maidens gay!

> Farewell, farewell! but this I tell
> To thee, thou Wedding-Guest!
> He prayeth well, who loveth well
> Both man and bird and beast.

We also read in *Hamlet* of a prayer hindered by sin. Polonius, behind the curtains, listens to the guilty King of Denmark as he endeavors to pray. The King says:

> O, my offence is rank, it smells to heaven;
> It hath the primal eldest curse upon 't,
> A brother's murder! — Pray can I not,
> Though inclination be as sharp as will:
> My stronger guilt defeats my strong intent.

Then he asks:

> But, O! what form of prayer
> Can serve my turn? Forgive me my foul murder! —
> That cannot be; since I am still possess'd
> Of those effects for which I did the murder.

At length, giving up the futile effort to pray, the King, rising from his knees, says:

> My words fly up, my thoughts remain below;
> Words without thoughts never to heaven go.

II. THE PRAYERS OF THE WICKED ARE NOT HEARD

There is another sense in which sin hinders prayer: it keeps God from hearing and answering our prayers. The insincere prayer is not heard and is not answered. We sincerely pray only for that which we sincerely desire in our hearts, and we do not really worship God until we desire to be what He would have us to be. That is why many of our prayers are unanswered. There is no sincere desire prompting them.

If I regard iniquity in my heart, the Psalmist said, *the Lord will not hear me.* We hear much about hypocrisy. The man who outwardly prays for deliverance from that which he inwardly retains and cherishes is indeed a hypocrite.

Even if God were willing to grant an answer to the man who prays, while at the same time he regards and retains sin in his heart, the blessing asked could do no good. How could the seed of love take root in the revengeful and hating heart? How could the seed of truth lodge in the false heart or the flower of virtue bloom in the unclean heart? The soul must be prepared to receive the blessing. If you go out on an April day and sow the seed, the summer fields will become white with harvest. But if you sow the seed in January or December, there will be no harvest. The blessings of God for which we ask are given to us without money and without price. Nevertheless, they are subject to certain laws and conditions, no less than the seed which produces the golden harvest.

Live, then, so as to be free from those sins which hinder your prayers and harm your spiritual life. Be sure that if you regard iniquity in your heart, God will not hear you. What is there in your heart now which makes you come so slowly to the place of prayer, or, when you kneel there, renders your utterance feeble and incoherent, or silences it altogether? What is there within that is not renounced, and yet ought to be? Rid your heart of these things, and then its channels will be open for the free and gracious flowing of the waters of prayer.

One who had once prayed for experience in prayer, but who had been regarding sin in his heart, and had known only unrest and distress until he renounced his sin and found peace, made this statement: "After a long time of jangling conflict and inner misery I one day, quietly, and with no conscious effort, stopped doing the disingenuous thing I had been doing. Then the marvel happened. It was as if a great rubber band, which had been stretched almost to the breaking point, were suddenly released and snapped back to its normal condition. Heaven and earth were changed for me. Everything was glorious because of its relation to some great central life. Nothing seemed to matter but that life."

One of the finest passages in Goethe's *Faust*, is that in which the lovely Margaret, in one of her meetings with her lover, expresses to Faust her repugnance for the companion whom he sometimes brings with him, Mephistopheles. Faust tells her that it is only an antipathy, but the innocent maid is sure that there is a reason for her loathing and horror, and she says that when he is at hand it is impossible for her to pray:

> It overcomes me in such degree
> That wheresoe'er he meets us,
> I feel as though I'd lost my love for thee.
> When he is by, I could not pray to heaven.
> That burns within me like a flame, and surely, Henry,
> 'Tis with thee the same.
>
> —*Faust*, Scene XVI

What is true of an evil companion is true also of the thoughts, purposes, meditations and desires which we take into our hearts. Occupied with them, our souls cannot lift themselves to God, and our hindered prayers fall back unanswered to the ground.

Prayer is the mightiest agency which man can employ, but it is also the most sensitive to insincerity, infidelity and sin. Let us strive so to live that if we have, as we shall have, prayers which are unanswered, the reason and the mystery shall be in God, and not in us.

V

DELAYED ANSWERS TO PRAYER

He abode two days still in the same place where he was (John 11:6)

He would not for a while (Luke 18:4)

DELAYED ANSWERS TO PRAYER

He abode two days still in the same place where he was
(John 11:6).

He would not for a while (Luke 18:4).

When Lazarus came home one evening from Jerusalem, he complained of not feeling well. Martha and Mary did what they could to relieve him, but in the morning he was worse. The local physician, or leech, was called in to apply his remedies, but with no success. Then the anxious sisters held a consultation. Lazarus was very ill. There was no doubt about that. Naturally, they thought of Him who loved Lazarus and who often had spent the night in their Bethany home. So a messenger was sent to Jesus, who was far away, in the country beyond the Jordan. When the messenger found Jesus he said, *He whom thou lovest is sick.* Jesus, when He heard this word, said, *This sickness is not unto death, but for the glory of God, that the Son of God might be glorified thereby.* Apparently, He meant that the final issue of the sickness of Lazarus would not be death, and that the subsequent history would be to the glory of God.

Immediately after the statement of John that Jesus loved Martha and her sister and Lazarus comes the strange verse introduced with a "Therefore." *When he had heard therefore that he was sick, he abode two days still in the same place where he was.* After two days He set out on His journey to Bethany.

Meanwhile, the anxious sisters were wondering why Jesus had not come. Had He received the message? Did He understand the serious nature of Lazarus' sickness? While one sister watched by his side, the other went to the top of the hill and looked down the winding white road which led from the east and the Jordan.

Several days passed, and Jesus did not come. At length, another messenger came — Death himself. On his way towards Bethany Jesus knew, either by divine intuition or through a second message, that Lazarus was dead. He spoke of him as "asleep"; but when His disciples did not understand, He told them plainly, *Lazarus is dead*.

When Jesus was a great distance from the house at Bethany, Martha came out to meet Him and with gentle expostulation said, *Lord, if thou hadst been here, my brother had not died*. As soon as Jesus reached the house, Mary came and, falling down at His feet, repeated the gentle reproach of her sister Martha. Full of sympathy for their sorrow (we are told that Jesus wept), Jesus went with the sisters to the grave and worked the great miracle of resurrection which brought Lazarus back to his sisters, and at the same time sealed His own fate, for it was when the Pharisees saw the effect of this miracle upon the people that they took counsel to put Him to death.

If thou hadst been here! How often that expression is in our minds or on our lips. We wonder, as those sisters must have wondered, at the strange delay of Jesus, until, so far as they could see, He had tarried too long.

I. BY PRECEPT AND BY EXAMPLE CHRIST TAUGHT THAT THERE WILL SOMETIMES BE LONG DELAYS IN THE ANSWERS TO OUR PRAYERS

If we interpret certain promises of Christ regarding prayer to mean that through our prayers we can have anything at any time, we err. We have the plain teaching of Jesus that there will be delays, and that sometimes the delays of God will seem as strange and needless as in the case of Lazarus.

In two great parables, that of the selfish neighbor and that of the unjust judge, Jesus teaches men to persevere, and not to faint, in their prayers. But He teaches also in these parables that there will be delays in God's response which will seem to us to indicate that He does not care, and is as unmindful of our necessities and our distresses as was the unjust judge who feared neither God nor man, and who finally avenged the widow of her adversary only to save himself the annoyance of her continual coming.

In the story of the Phoenician woman, whose daughter was possessed of a devil, Christ by His own example illustrates the delays of God and the necessity of persevering earnestness in our prayers. When the woman first cried to Jesus to heal her daughter, He was silent. *He answered her not a word*. Then, when she continued her intercession, to the great irritation of the disciples, who besought Jesus to send her away, the Lord told the woman that He was not sent to any but the lost sheep of Israel. That is, His healing mission could not at that time include foreigners. But the woman was not to be discouraged, and, with tears streaming down her face, she asked Jesus to heal her daughter. This time Jesus gives a reply that seems even more severe than what He had said before. He said it was not appropriate to take the children's meat and give it to dogs. But the eager soul responded, *Truth, Lord, yet the dogs eat of the crumbs which fall from their masters' table*. Then Jesus, stirred to the depths by such persevering prayer, overcoming all obstacles, prayer that would take no denial, exclaimed, *O woman, great is thy faith! Be it unto thee, even as thou wilt*.

II. THE PURPOSE OF GOD WHEN HE DELAYS IN ANSWERING OUR PRAYERS

Everyone who is faithful in prayer will be able to point to his own unanswered prayers. As to God's purpose in His delays, we have nothing to guide us save His own words and the story of His delays recorded in the Bible. But we can say that if our prayers were all answered, and at once, our attitude towards God and the unseen world would be greatly changed, and that unfavorably. A man would not remain humble and trusting, but would become proud and self-reliant, if his every petition were granted at once.

The delays of God also teach us to search our hearts and lives and make sure that the cause of the delay and the silence of God is not in ourselves. If we regard iniquity in our hearts, the Lord will not hear us. No promise of God neutralizes His commandments. A king once presented to a favorite a gold ring, with the promise that whenever he presented it his request would be granted. This man committed a great crime, and when sentenced to death, he appealed to the king and showed him the gold ring. But the king ordered him to be hanged at once. No promise of God can be taken without the accompanying qualification of what He has said concerning sincerity of purpose and of life.

Some years ago I had a conversation with a minister whose classmate at Yale College was a man who afterwards became a useful and distinguished minister in the Presbyterian Church. When they were at Yale, the college was shaken with a revival, and nearly everyone was converted but this classmate, who seemed unresponsive to every appeal and unmoved by every prayer on his behalf. Years afterward, when he was in the ministry, he told his friend how it had happened. He was the son of godly parents who had prayed earnestly for his salvation. He said he was not unmoved, but, on the contrary, was greatly stirred by the revival at Yale. But he steeled himself against surrendering to the will of the Holy Spirit, chiefly because he felt that if he were converted he would have to become a minister. When he left college he was associated in Georgia with a well-known lawyer, and was advancing rapidly in his chosen profession. He had maintained little contact with his family, till one day he received a letter from a sister telling him of his mother's death and that she and his father had wanted him to know that she had died praying for his salvation. This message brought him to himself, and, going out into the forest, he fought his battle through to the end, made a complete surrender to God, relinquished his promising career at the bar, entered the theological seminary and in due time became a minister of the Gospel. Before he was licensed and ordained in the little church which he was supplying, there was to be a baptismal service. He invited an old minister, a friend of his father and mother, to administer the sacrament. Before he did so, the minister said that he recalled a scene which had taken place many years ago, when a handsome father with a beautiful wife at his side came up the aisle of the church to present their little child for baptism. When he asked for the name of the child, the mother gave him a slip of paper on which was written the child's name and the date of his birth, and underneath were these words: "Given to God and the Gospel ministry." "That child," said the minister, "is your pastor today."

The earnest, effectual prayer of a righteous mother availeth much. It is a blessed privilege to have a child for the salvation of whose soul you can pray. Even prayers which are in this world unanswered, may be answered. Answered or unanswered, such prayers are strength and riches for the soul. John Bunyan put these words in the mouth of Mr. Badman's wife, who was extremely troubled because of the unregenerate state of her husband: "Are my prayers lost? Are they forgotten? Are they thrown over the bar? No! They are hanged upon the horns of the Golden Altar, and I must have the benefit of them myself, that moment that I shall enter the gate in at which the righteous nation that keepeth truth shall enter. My prayers are not lost. My tears are yet in God's bottle."

In his *Confessions*, St. Augustine relates how he set out

for Rome from Carthage in opposition to the prayers and entreaties of his godly mother, who was praying earnestly for his salvation. Augustine deceived her when she was weeping over him by telling her that he was merely going on board the ship to see a friend who was going to sail for Italy. When his mother refused to go home without him, he persuaded her to pass the night in a memorial chapel of the martyr Cyprian. But that night, while his mother Monica was praying in the chapel and beseeching God to prevent him from going, Augustine set sail. This departure of her son must have seemed to Monica, at that time, the refusal to grant her prayer, yet in the providence of God that journey to Italy was to be the means of Augustine's conversion. The denial of the mother's prayer was, in the end, a great answer to her prayer for the salvation of her gifted son. "But Thou," says Augustine, "in Thy hidden wisdom, didst grant the substance of her desire, yet refused the thing she prayed for in order that Thou mightest effect in me what she was ever praying for . . . She loved to keep me with her as mothers are wont, yes, far more than most mothers, and she knew not what joy Thou wast preparing for her out of my desertion."

Here we have a striking and beautiful illustration of how God sometimes answers a prayer for the salvation of a soul after what seems a long delay to the one who made the request.

In one of His parables, teaching us to pray and not to faint, Jesus tells of the man who went at midnight to knock on his neighbor's door. What a picture that is! Often those who believe and who pray, must go at midnight, through darkness and silence, to knock on the door of Omnipotence. In your darkest midnight hours remember that parable, and grope your way to the door of God.

Man is endued with great powers, and none is more wonderful than this: he has power to help God answer prayer.

There are many unanswered prayers. Some of you fathers and mothers have prayed long and patiently. Perhaps your friends passed out of this world with no sign that their prayers were answered or would be answered. Let me now conclude by speaking to you for whom others have prayed and are praying at this very hour. Will you help God by your own repentance and faith to answer those prayers?

VI
PRAYER FOR OTHERS

Making mention of thee always in my prayers
(Philem. 4)

VI

PRAYER FOR OTHERS

Making mention of thee always in my prayers (Philem. 4).

You are indeed fortunate if you have a friend, a good man or a good woman, who is accustomed to make mention of you in his prayers at the Throne of Grace.

Well do I recall the Sabbath in December, 1922, when I ascended the pulpit stairs in the Arch Street Church in Philadelphia and realized that for the first time in my ministry, since my ordination, I had mounted the pulpit without the knowledge that our mother had been praying that day for her sons in the ministry. Perhaps, however, those who have passed within the veil are still permitted to remember us in their petitions.

One of the most beautiful poems I have ever read on the subject of prayer is one which I found in a Norwegian novel, *The Wind from the Mountains.* Adelaide hands to old Dag, who amid his sorrow and difficulties is struggling toward the light, the Bishop's Bible. These lines are on the flyleaf:

> Our human thoughts and works are not so mighty
> That they can cut a path to God unblessed,
> And so from Him the gift of prayer is sent us
> To hallow both our labor and our quest.
> Over life and death and starlit spaces,
> The high road runs, that at His word was laid,
> And reaches Him across the desert places;
> By prayer it is our pilgrimage is made.

How true that is! Over life and death and starlit spaces runs the high road of prayer, and by prayer our pilgrimage is made. When the Atlantic cable was laid in 1866 there were great celebrations, illuminations and bonfires; there was the firing of cannon on both sides of the Atlantic. But what was the Atlantic cable, or what today is that more wonderful accomplishment which links together the continents, the wireless and the radio, compared with the soul's great radio and wireless of prayer, whereby we have immediate communication with heaven and whereby we can contact with the fervent desires and thoughts of our hearts not merely many millions, as Roosevelt and Churchill do, but all mankind?

Too often our prayers are motivated by a desire to fulfill our own wishes and desires. But the noblest type of prayer is prayer for others. The first prayer recorded in the Bible, the prayer of Abraham, was a prayer for others: his intercession for the cities of the plain. The last words of Christ to His disciples before His crucifixion was a prayer that they might be kept in the Truth and from the evil that is in the world. Paul, when he knelt on the sands of Miletus, having finished all his ministry for the church at Ephesus, poured out his soul in intercession for the elders of that church.

I. THE BENEFITS OF PRAYER FOR OTHERS

These benefits are seen, first of all, in the reaction of him who prays. Such prayer lifts the man who prays out of himself and brings to view the glories of life. Paul spoke of the joy he had in praying for others. To his favorite church, the church at Philippi, he wrote: *Always in every prayer of mine for you all making request with joy.* Our Saviour said that *it is more blessed to give than to receive,* and one realizes the truth of those words when he kneels at the Golden Altar of intercession for others. Prayer for others widens and extends the horizon of the soul. It waters and irrigates the life with Christian love.

The second benefit of prayer for others is the benefit it bestows upon those for whom we pray. To pray for another is to show him the highest loyalty and deepest affection. Paul said of the Philippian Christians, *I have you always in my heart.* To pray for another is to show the purest interest in another's welfare and to do him the highest service. When

Lord Byron received word that a devout woman, who had recently died, had offered a petition on his behalf, praying for his salvation, he wrote to the husband: "I can assure you that not all the fame which ever cheated humanity into higher notions of its own importance would ever weigh in my mind against the pure and pious interest which a virtuous being may be pleased to take in my behalf. In this point of view I would not exchange the prayer of the deceased in my behalf for the united glory of Homer, Caesar and Napoleon."

There are some who like to believe — and it is indeed a pleasant thought — that there are guardian angels who attend our spirits. Whether that be true or not, the one who prays for another is, as it were, a guardian angel for that soul. There are on record, too, some very striking and impressive accounts of how people were saved from physical or moral disaster, and afterwards learned that at the very time that their bodies or souls were in danger, one who loved them had been praying for them.

II. PRAYING FOR ENEMIES

That was a new element in the teaching of Jesus. Sulla boasted that no one had done more good to his friends or more harm to his enemies than he. But Jesus introduced a new way of dealing with our enemies; He said that we should pray for them. Christ commanded, *Love your enemies, bless them that curse you, do good to them that hate you, and pray for them that despitefully use you, and persecute you; that ye may be the children of your Father which is in heaven.*

Madame Chiang Kai-shek, who is a product of Christian missions and whose father and mother were devout Methodists, relates that her mother spent hours in prayer in a room on the third floor of their home. At the time of the Manchurian invasion, Madame Chiang Kai-shek said one day to her mother: "Mother, you are so powerful in prayer, why don't you pray that God will annihilate Japan by an earthquake or something?" Her mother looked gravely at her and said, "When you pray or expect me to pray, don't insult God's intelligence by asking Him to do something which would be unworthy of you, a mortal." "After that," said Madame Chiang, "I can pray for the Japanese people."

It is not pleasant to think of those who dislike you or who have wronged you or hurt you. But such persons are often in your life, and much depends upon the way in which you deal with them. The best way to deal with them is by prayer. It is hard to hate anyone after you have prayed for him. In the Bible we have beautiful examples of noble men who prayed for their enemies. Samuel was deeply hurt when the people asked for a king because his sons were evil men and he himself was getting old, but he ended his long leadership of the people of Israel with a promise that he would pray for them. *God forbid,* he said, *that I should sin against the Lord in ceasing to pray for you.* In the New Testament we read of Stephen who, when wicked men were stoning him to death outside the walls of Jerusalem, prayed, *Lord, lay not this sin to their charge.* When he had said this he fell asleep.

When Joseph Parker, the great London preacher of the last century, was debating one day on the town green with enemies of Christianity, an infidel shouted at him, "What did Christ do for Stephen when he was stoned?" Parker answered — and he said the answer was given him like an inspiration from heaven — "He gave him grace to pray for those who stoned him." It was the belief of St. Augustine and of Luther that the prayer which was offered by Stephen for those who stoned him, and which Paul must have heard when he held the clothes of those who did the stoning, was used of God for the conversion of the apostle.

Sublimest of all was that prayer which our Saviour prayed

when His enemies were nailing Him to the bitter Cross:
Father, forgive them, for they know not what they do.

III. PRAYER FOR THE SALVATION OF ANOTHER SOUL

This is the greatest gift one can request in behalf of another soul. Some time ago I was asked this question: "Can
a soul that has been prayed for be lost?" The questioner
cited these two passages from the Bible: I John 5:14, *And
this is the confidence that we have in him, that if we ask any
thing according to his will, he heareth us,* and II Samuel
14:14, *Yet doth God devise means that his banished be not
expelled from him.* This text refers to the plan which the
woman of Tekoah suggested to David by which he could
recall his banished son Absalom.

This question showed true Christian faith on the part of
the one who asked it. Where there is genuine Christian
faith, there is also deep concern for the salvation of others.
The one who asked the question also showed his faith in the
solemn teachings of the Bible, that man by nature is a sinner,
that he needs salvation and that Christ is the only Saviour.
The passage which he mentioned is one that ought to give
us great confidence when we pray for the salvation of another soul. John says, *If we ask any thing according to
his will, he heareth us.* There is nothing that could be more
in accordance with the will of God than the salvation of an
immortal soul; thus the questioner was prompted to ask,
"Can a soul that has been prayed for be lost?" God, we know,
is not willing that any should perish. The Bible resounds
with the deep and tender longing of God for man's salvation.
God is not willing that any should perish, but that all should
come to the knowledge of salvation; and He was so unwilling
that anyone should be lost that He gave His only begotten
Son, that whosoever believeth in Him might not perish but
have everlasting life.

Yet this confidence in the prayer for the salvation of a

soul must be related to those conditions of salvation which are made plain in the Scriptures. There is, first of all, the question of man's own will. God has made man with the solemn power of choice. He can resist the will of God or he can obey it. It is only by doing the will of God that man can accept Jesus Christ and be saved. There is a difference between what God desires and what He wills by decree. He desires that all men should be saved. He wills that they shall be saved by repentance and faith in Jesus Christ. No prayer can change the plan of God, and there can be no salvation against the will of the soul that is saved. What we really pray for, then, when we pray for the salvation of another soul, is not that, regardless of his life, which perhaps is ungodly, or his faith, which perhaps does not exist, the man may be saved, but that he may be moved by the Holy Spirit to do the will of God and believe on Jesus Christ unto eternal life. It is the will of God for each one of you that you should be saved through repentance and through faith in Jesus Christ. Will you do the will of God?

With these considerations in mind, we can have great confidence in prayer for the salvation of another soul. When Monica, the mother of St. Augustine, wearied the Bishop of Hippo with her intercessions and continual coming in behalf of her wayward boy, he cried out impatiently one day, "Woman, go thy way! It is impossible that the child of so many prayers should be lost!"

A mother's prayers are one of the mightiest influences in this universe. The gifted Stephen Phillips, who led a wayward life and died a sad death, but left behind him such noble poems as "Nero," "Herod" and "The Sin of David," had a godly, praying mother, and in one of his better moments he expressed in these words his hope that his mother's prayers would result in his final salvation. I think that by giving expression to such a hope he showed that he was on the way to true repentance and faith:

O mother, that from thy pure heart each night
Sendest up thy prayers for me to highest God;
For me, who wander without fixed light,
And have not faith to tread where thou has trod;
Grieve not, though God no answer yet hath given;
He knows that mine is not a lasting doom;
Though thou be caught up into highest heaven,
And I be banished into outer gloom;
For then the aching absence of thy face
Shall work in me such swift immortal pain
That I shall struggle through the worlds of space
In burning hope to be with thee again.
And I shall strive for thy white purity
For fear of everlasting losing thee.

We can have great hope that a child of the Covenant, one given to God by believing parents in the waters of baptism, and for whose salvation earnest prayers have been offered, will be brought at last to saving faith and into the kingdom of heaven. The mother of the famous preacher, T. DeWitt Talmage, when she led the prayers at family worship, often prayed, "O Lord God, I ask not for my children wealth or honor, but I do ask that they all may be subjects of Thy converting grace." That is the ideal prayer for every Christian mother.

When you pray for another's soul, you take your stand by the side of the great Intercessor Himself, our Lord and Saviour Jesus Christ. We know that in the days of His flesh Christ was a man of prayer. He prayed on the mountain, when He was transfigured, in the desert place before the dawn, and at the Last Supper, when He prayed for the disciples. But that is not the last record of the intercessory prayers of Christ. The inspired writers of the New Testament tell us that the present occupation of our Saviour is intercession. Paul says, *It is Christ that died, yea rather, that is risen again, who is even at the right hand of God, who also maketh intercession for us . . . He is able also to save to the uttermost them that come unto God by him, seeing he ever liveth to make intercession for them.*

Remember that Christ, the Son of God, prays for you. The

Lord Jesus Christ, who uttered His groans and His sighs, and poured out His tears and His blood upon the Cross for your salvation, prays for you. *He ever liveth to make intercession for [you].* When you are sad or heavy-hearted or lonely, remember that Christ prays for you. When you are tempted, remember that Christ is praying for you. When you are faint-hearted and discouraged by the way, remember that your Friend and Saviour is praying for you. When you are cast down and smitten with remorse because of your failure and your sin, remember that you have a great Friend. You have the Greatest Lover of them all, your Saviour Jesus Christ, who loved you and died for you, and now intercedes for you. Remember what He said to Peter, so soon to **fall**: *But I have prayed for thee, that thy faith fail not.*

VII
THE PROFIT OF PRAYER

What is the Almighty, that we should serve him?
and what profit should we have, if we pray unto
him? (Job 21:15)

THE PROFIT OF PRAYER

What is the Almighty, that we should serve him? and what profit
should we have, if we pray unto him? (Job 21:15).

When Grant was fighting his last campaign against cancer
at Mt. McGregor, General O. O. Howard, who had honestly
won the title "the Christian soldier," came to call on him.
He spoke for a time to Grant about some of the battles and
campaigns of the war in which both men had played so
illustrious a part. Grant listened for a time, and then, inter-
rupting him, said, "Howard, tell me what you know about
prayer." Face to face with death and the unknown, the dying
soldier was more interested in prayer than in the reminis-
cences of his battles.

Troubled Job had been speaking of the prosperity of the
wicked: their houses were safe from fear; the rod of God
was not upon them. *Their seed is established in their sight
with them, and their offspring before their eyes. Their
houses are safe from fear, neither is the rod of God upon
them. Their bull gendereth, and faileth not; their cow
calveth, and casteth not her calf. They send forth their little
ones like a flock, and their children dance. They take the
timbrel and harp, and rejoice at the sound of the organ* (Job
21:8-12).

This fortified prosperity led them to trust in their own
strength, and in their pride and arrogancy they forgot God.
"Who is God, anyway?" they asked. "Can you see Him? Can
you hear Him? What is the use of praying to Him? Our
flocks have multiplied, our fields have brought forth their
increase, and our families have been saved from disease and
death; yet we have not served God or prayed to Him."

These men made a double mistake. First of all, they as-
sumed that their present worldly condition was a permanent

71

one. Job corrected that by his famous metaphor: *How oft is the candle of the wicked put out!* A single breath of wind, and lo, the prosperity of the wicked vanishes. The second mistake was this: they thought that herds and bursting barns and numerous progeny constituted the sole or the greatest blessing in life. Without God a man may amass a fortune in this world, although even in things material the fear of God is often the foundation of prosperity. But the Bible makes it plain that a man can be rich toward this world and yet poor toward God.

Let us turn from the problem of the prosperity of the wicked to the questions asked by these prosperous atheists: "What profit will we have if we pray to Him? Does prayer do anything? Is it worth our thought and effort and constant observation?"

Earnest prayer always lifts the mind and ennobles the heart because it brings man into the presence of God. In his *Twilight of Christianity*, Harry Elmer Barnes says: "The preposterous assumptions underlying the orthodox notions of prayer have led nearly all Modernists to concede the improbability or indeed the impossibility of effecting God's will or the course of events through prayer. They have rested content with the effort to justify prayer on the ground of its beneficial effect upon the mind of the communicant." No evangelical Christian holds such a view of prayer or its limitations. He believes that even in the physical and natural world, as the Bible repeatedly illustrates, the fervent, effectual prayer of a righteous man availeth much. Nevertheless, the influence of prayer upon the life of him who prays is very great. It was as He was praying that the face of Jesus was transfigured. So prayer, though in a far different sense, transfigures the face of him who engages in it. Even the memory of past seasons of prayer remains with one for many years and comes back to him to speak a word of encouragement or warning in time of trial.

In his *Up from Methodism*, Herbert Asbury gives an extraordinary picture of family worship in the house of his godly uncle. At the conclusion of this amazing caricature, he says: "Every night, year after year, this sort of thing went on in houses all over Farmington, and for that matter, all over the United States. It would be interesting to know how many hours were wasted in the course of a year by such senseless appeals to the Heavenly Father."

I have no doubt that there are many in the Church who could rise up to testify in a far different note. Your thoughts travel back to the home of your childhood, and even now you can hear the accents of your parents' voices as they knelt at the family altar, commended their children to God and pleaded for the salvation of their souls.

Prayer reveals the sacredness of life. In prayer I come face to face with my soul, and there I behold in that brief moment of retirement from the world's rush and glare the grand possibilities of life. In the light which streams from the Golden Altar, I can see not only the weakness of my life, but also its possible and divinely intended greatness. Our own prayers for ourselves, the prayers of others for us and Christ's prayers on our behalf, even as He prayed for Peter — these prayers invest each one of us with a sacred interest and remind us that we have a never-dying soul to save.

Prayer unmasks and discovers temptation. Temptation, to be successful, must have a degree of plausibility and reasonableness. It wears the fair mask of profit or pleasure. Prayer strips this mask from the face of temptation. Prayer is no substitute for conscience, yet it always clears the atmosphere of those clouds and mists which sometimes hover low about the path of duty. It is sometimes said that the incitement to evil in the world is stronger than the incitement to good. That is expressed in the following lines:

They say that poison-sprinkled flowers
Are sweeter in perfume
Than when, untouched by deadly dew,
They glowed in early bloom.

They say that men condemned to die
Have quaffed the sweetened wine
With higher relish than the juice
Of the untempered vine.

And I believe the Devil's voice
Sinks deeper in our ear
Than any whisper sent from heaven,
However sweet and clear.

When we consider the weakness of human nature under temptation and the moral breakdowns and the shipwrecks which occur when least expected, we are inclined to feel that these lines are true, and that the Devil's voice has more power with the soul than the whisper sent from heaven. Yet we cannot forget the clear utterance of the voice of conscience, heard when we pray. Satan is powerless to harm a man when he is on his knees. When Satan gets him far away from the Golden Altar, he attacks. There are actions, attitudes, desires, purposes and dreams which cannot stand the test of the altar of prayer. There would be less sin in the world if there were more prayer.

Prayer helps us in our struggle against temptation. It not only undeceives the tempted, but it puts a weapon in his hand. When I see the crowds of humanity pouring like a vast river down the canyons of our city streets, wearing on their faces the marks of sorrow, anxiety, care, pleasure, passion and hope, I sometimes ask myself how many of these have fortified themselves against the day's dangers and temptations by a brief moment of prayer before they started out in the morning. If more did so, there would be fewer falls, failures and shipwrecks.

A medical missionary, captured by bandits in China, and informed that he was to be shot in ten minutes, tells how a terrible fear and helplessness came over him at the thought of dying so far away from his native country, his friends and his family. But he had strength enough to pray. This was his prayer: "My Lord God, have mercy on me, and give me strength for this trial. Take away all fear, and if I have to die, let me die like a man." Instantly, he says, his terrible fear began to disappear. By the time he had reached the gorge where he was to be shot he felt perfectly calm and unafraid. In the days which followed, full of danger and suffering, the memory of this experience was cherished more and more. "My own will had failed in the most critical moment of my life. But the knowledge that I could depend on a power greater than my own, one that had not failed me in that crisis, sustained me in a wonderful way to the very end of my captivity. What ingratitude it would be in me not to proclaim this power."

In that crisis, prayer linked his soul with God, and his strength was made perfect in weakness. Multitudes have found this to be true. By faith we can believe that prayers dealing with problems in the natural world have been answered. But we can never prove that a prayer for rain or the healing of disease has been answered, for there are natural laws at work. But when we find ourselves making progress in patience, self-control, kindness and purity, we can be sure that prayer is being answered, because there are no natural forces operative in the realm of the moral and spiritual. Whatever is accomplished in that sphere must be of God. When the bandits of life, such as Fear, Hate, Revenge and Lust lay hold on us, prayer gives us courage to face them unafraid and in full confidence that God will deliver us. When we pray, we put the eternal resources on our side. When Christ prayed in Gethsemane, a great angel came to strengthen Him. That angel has never had his commission withdrawn. Still he comes to strengthen those who pray.

One of the greatest truths concerning prayer is this: it is *never too late to pray.* Prayer is not only the highest resource of the soul, but it is the last. No matter what the neglects, failures, blunders, sufferings, sins and sorrows of yesterday, today the greatest thing is still possible — prayer.

> Lord, what a change within us one short hour
> Spent in Thy presence will prevail to make;
> What heavy burdens from our bosoms take;
> What parched grounds refresh as with a shower!
> We kneel — and all about us seems to lower;
> We rise — and all, the distant and the near,
> Stands forth in sunny outline, brave and clear.
> We kneel, how weak! we rise, how full of power!
> Why, therefore, should we do ourselves this wrong,
> Or others, that we are not always strong;
> That we are ever overborne with care,
> Anxious and troubled, when with us is prayer,
> And joy and strength and courage are with Thee?

VIII
PRAYER AND TEMPTATION

Watch and pray, that ye enter not into temptation
(Matt. 26:41)

PRAYER AND TEMPTATION

Watch and pray, that ye enter not into temptation (Matt. 26:41).

From the steeple of St. Mary's Church in Cracow, Poland, a bugle has been sounded every day for the last seven hundred years. The last note on the bugle is always half muted and broken, as if some disaster had befallen the bugler. This seven-hundred-year commemoration is in memory of a heroic trumpeter who one night sounded a blast on his trumpet and summoned the people to defend their city against the hordes of the invading Tartars. As he was sounding the last blast of his trumpet, an arrow shot by one of the Tartars struck him and killed him. This is the reason for the muffled note at the end.

When I read these familiar words in the three Gospels, *Watch ye and pray, lest ye enter into temptation,* I am reminded of the fact that Christ was a faithful Bugler for our souls. Through the ages He has sounded His bugle, warning His disciples, and you and me today, against the power of temptation. Like the bugler on the tower of that church in Poland who died as he sounded the warning on his trumpet, so Christ died as He sounded forth this never to be silenced warning for our souls. Indeed, from the three sacred narratives we can be certain that even as He spoke these words to His disciples, the marks of the bloody sweat were upon His brow.

Only Christ knew the value of a human soul. Only Christ knew all Satan's devices and his malignant desire to sift our souls as wheat. The value that Christ put upon your soul is expressed in that bloody struggle in Gethsemane's shadows, and in that tragic and lonely death on Calvary's tree.

When Christ said to His disciples, *Watch ye and pray, lest ye enter into temptation,* He did not mean, of course, that we are merely to pray that we may be kept from temptation, for Christ Himself was tempted as we are. It was His desire that in temptation we might not be destroyed. Half of those who are destroyed by temptation are first of all destroyed by being deceived. A man once watched an Indian prepare a snare with a noose with which to catch a wild animal. He was surprised to learn that the Indian never sprung the trap or pulled the noose the first time that the animal appeared. Instead, he let it come repeatedly and feed where the trap was, and then, when the animal had become bold and thoroughly familiar with the surroundings, the Indian set the trap so that the next time it came the animal would be caught in the snare. That is the way temptation works. It does not drive its shaft into the heart of its victim immediately, but deceives it and lures it on, and then the fatal blow is delivered.

Temptation is a universal fact. There are temptations of the body, temptations of the mind, temptations of the spirit. Temptation is a great equalizer. There is grim democracy and communism in temptation. Temptation smites in youth; it smites in middle life; even the aged are not exempt from its cruel and dangerous sorrows, for —

> The gray-haired saint may fall at last,
> The surest guide a wanderer prove;
> Death only binds us fast
> To that bright shore of love.

Temptation is a sleepless, unwearying enemy. The Scotch-Irish forefathers who settled and conquered the wilderness of Western Pennsylvania, as they went about their daily toil, cleared the forests and cultivated the fields, were ever mindful of the fact that there was a cruel, crafty, merciless and bloodthirsty foe always lurking about, waiting for an opportunity to find the settler off his guard and eager to fire the fatal shot or hurl his tomahawk and rush forward with the encircling knife. So, although men are often supinely oblivious of it, you and I have an enemy who is watching and waiting to find us off our guard; his patience is never exhausted, and his enmity is unsleeping. How powerful a figure is that used by our Lord when He spoke to Cain, warning him against the temptation of hatred and jealousy that at length moved him to his dreadful crime: *Sin croucheth at the door*. The figure is that of a wild animal, flattened against the ground, a rock, or the limb of a tree, watching and waiting to make his fatal spring.

Great is the power of temptation, and great is the destructive power of a single temptation. One of the old fathers used to stand in awe of what the angel said to Tobias, namely, that temptation was necessary for the purification of his soul. *If,* he thought, *temptation was necessary for a saint like Tobias, then how much more necessary it is for me, and how much greater its power will be!* There are many facts about temptation which may well make a man stand in awe; an outstanding one is this: a single temptation not fought against with the divinely appointed weapon can ruin a character that has been slowly and painfully built through long years.

The witness of your own soul will confirm that Christ is not warning us against an imaginary danger when He warns us against temptation. In this fight with temptation He says there is only one weapon to use, and that is *prayer. Watch ye and pray, lest ye enter into* [*that is, be conquered by*] *temptation*. There is no essential difference here between watching and praying; they are not two separate things. Indeed, the narrative in Luke says, *RISE and pray, lest ye enter into temptation*. When a man is really watching against temptation he is praying against it, and when he is praying against it he is watching against it in the highest sense of the word.

I have often wondered what happened to a young woman whom I knew. Did she follow the counsel given her? Did she obey the voice that spoke when she prayed, and, turning her back on the temptation forever, did she henceforth follow the path of rectitude and honor and the highest happiness? Or, did she disregard the advice she was given and which she had sought, and fail to heed the clear voice of direction that spoke to her when she prayed, and follow instead the suggestion of a soul without honor? That I have wondered, not only concerning her, but concerning many others. In the years which have passed since that time, I have often thought of her reply which she gave when I asked her a question: "Oh, then it seems to be wrong!"

This is an example taken from life, and by it I wish to show the power, the helpfulness and the fidelity of prayer. The young woman whom I mentioned was attractive and evidently intelligent. What she told me and asked me did not amaze me nor shock me. I was, however, somewhat surprised that there was in her mind uncertainty as to the right or wrong of the proposed action. Today, having dealt with several similar cases since that time, I must confess that I would not be surprised even at such apparent lack of certainty as to the right or wrong of what was contemplated.

This young woman was a student in one of the medical colleges of Philadelphia. While in the city she had become acquainted with a young man, and between them there had sprung up a close relationship. They shared what was, or what they took to be, a sincere affection. Out of their friendship there came a proposal as to a course of action. What was proposed was unusual, at least, unconventional, and would have been regarded with amazement and indignation. But before she committed herself to this course of action, something had made her hesitate. Perhaps it was the influence of her early religious training. She had consulted one of her instructors at the medical college, who, dealing with the subject in the abstract rather than in the concrete, seemed to sanction what had been proposed. Yet she was not satisfied. Therefore, she had come to inquire what the Bible and the Church, the representative of religion, said regarding the subject.

When I learned that she had been reared as a Christian, I said to her, "Then you know the Ten Commandments?" She answered that she did. "Don't you know that what you propose is contrary to one of those commandments, and, therefore, sinful?" She replied that she was not sure that it was sinful. If she had been sure, she would not have consulted me. This perplexed me a little. I said to her, "Do you ever pray about it?" She answered, "Yes." "How did it seem to you then?" "Oh, then," was her immediate answer, "it seemed to be wrong." "Then," I said, "if I were you, I would follow the verdict of your prayer. Since your own prayer told you that it was wrong, it was not necessary to consult me, for you already had the advice of a far wiser Counselor and Friend."

Then she left. Did she act upon the advice which I had given her, or, rather, which I had drawn from the depths of her own conscience? Did she cease to question the sinfulness of the action proposed? Or, like many another, did she refuse to obey the verdict of her prayers? Has she been sucked down into the maelstrom of sin and sorrow, that gulf which shows no mercy, heeds no cries and sweeps remorselessly over the soul which it has submerged? Of all that I know nothing. But her quick response when I asked her, "How did it seem when you prayed about it?" often comes back to me. Prayer had done its true and grand part. It had showed her the danger and the sinfulness of what she was tempted to do.

THE TEMPTATION OF A FRIEND

This young woman was tempted by a friend, one of the most dangerous forms of temptation. In a letter written to me after I had preached a sermon on temptation was this sentence: "The one we regard as 'a bad actor' rarely gets close enough to us to influence us or to do us harm. It is the 'nice person' that may prove to be our stumbling block, if we are not on our guard." Temptation never comes as a devil, but always in most attractive form, as that which appeals to us most, is most admired, is most desired. This was certainly so in the case of the young woman. Friendship, a desire to please and, even more, affection, may serve to disguise the native blackness and hideousness of temptation and sin. Christ said to the Devil, *Get thee behind me, Satan*; He said this not only to the Devil but to his best friend, and the chief of the apostles, Peter. The friend of the young woman whom I mentioned was a poor, wretched, degraded and dishonorable friend, and his proposal was worthy only of her scorn and detestation. Nevertheless, it came from one who seemed to be a sincere friend, and that in itself gave a degree of plausibility to the proposal. That temptation is most to be feared which mingles good with evil.

> Oftentimes to win us to our harm,
> The instruments of darkness tell us truths,
> Win us with honest trifles, to betray us
> In deepest consequences.
>
> *—Macbeth*

Had this suggestion come from anyone but a friend, it would at once have been indignantly repudiated and dismissed. "He had a friend," or "She had a friend," is an epitaph that might well be placed upon the grave of many a man or woman.

The fact that this woman came to see me indicated her realization that the decision she made would have an important influence upon her life. She felt, however dimly, that she was at a turning of the path, and that her choice in that moment would bring her either strength and satisfaction or sorrow and misery. This solemn mystery of choice envelopes every human life. The moral history of man is prefigured for us in the story of man's fall. So race after race, age after age, individual after individual, is called upon to make a decision between right and wrong. What capacities for either happiness or misery every human breast has locked within it!

Prayer did not fail on this occasion. When I asked the young woman, "Do you ever pray about it?" I would not have been greatly surprised had she replied that she did not; but when she confessed that she did pray about it, I had no misgiving whatever as to what her answer would be when I said to her, "How did it seem to you then?" Prayer, like the wind which sweeps away the fog at sea, never fails to reveal the headlands and promontories of the moral world. It reveals to man his eternal interests.

THE VALUE OF PRAYER

He was a well dressed young man. When he came into my study I thought he had come to sell me something, and I waited for him to state his mission. But I found that he had come on an altogether different errand. He was a young man of good position, of excellent education, background and family. He was the son of a clergyman. He told me of his struggle with an evil appetite, the damage that it had already wrought in his life, and his fear that it would do him even greater injury in the future. It was not necessary for me to point out the reality of the temptation or the sinfulness of what he was tempted to do. Already he realized that to the full. He was beginning to find strength and help in prayer, and sought help, not only guidance as to his own prayers but he desired the prayers of others. He came not only to speak about his difficulty, but to have the association of intercession. When he rose to go, he said to me, "I am the son of a minister, and I was reared in a Christian home, yet I never used to believe in prayer; but now I begin to see that there is something in it."

What had he begun to see and to find in prayer? One

thing he had found: prayer revealed to him the greatness and the value of his soul. If he yielded to the temptation which was besetting him, he knew that this would result in tragedy, and that the degradation of his soul was the greatest injury which could befall him. Much has been accomplished when that has been made clear. It is when we realize that we have something of infinite value within us that we are prepared to defend it against the assault of the Devil. That was the way the Hebrew lad felt in the palace of Potiphar when he cried, *How then can I do this great wickedness, and sin against God?* By showing a man the importance of what is involved, prayer strengthens his arm for resistance and enables him to continue the fight. Satan has no difficult task with a man who meets him without prayer, but the Devil knows he must wage war when he tries to drag down a soul which defends itself with the armor of prayer. There is a gripping truth in the couplet from the old hymn:

> Satan trembles when he sees
> The weakest saint upon his knees.

Yes, those words are true, mysteriously, grandly true. The weakest saint upon his knees is armed with a weapon that Satan dreads beyond all else. Satan, great enemy of man's soul, see what you can do with a man who prays. You can do nothing with him! You know that you can do nothing with him, for he is on his knees. He is armed with prayer! The great business, then, of Satan, is to tempt men to rise from their knees and neglect to pray. But when a man prays, Satan has no power over him.

> I know of a land that knows a lord
>   That's neither brave nor true;
> But I know of a sword, a sword, a sword,
>   Can cut a chain in two.
> Its edge is sharp and its blade is broad.
>   I know of a sword, a sword, a sword
>   Will cut a chain in two.

When the pilot of a plane gets into the mists or the cloud banks, what does he do? He drives the plane above the clouds; he soars where sun or moon or stars are shining and the atmosphere is cold and clear. When the mists and fogs of temptation gather about a soul, it must *climb*. How can it climb? By that marvelous device, more wonderful than any ever invented by man's mind — *prayer*. Prayer is the great upward movement of the soul. It lifts you above the clouds.

Once when flying across the continent I saw one of the most beautiful sights that I ever expect to see. The clouds drifted beneath our airship, and the light of the morning sun shone on them. I shall never forget that beauty. But there is something more beautiful than that. When a soul which has overcome temptation by prayer and has risen above it, looks down in triumph upon the conquered foe, that is indeed beautiful.

There was once a king whose enemy tried to poison him. He arranged that the king should be handed a cup of wine into which poison had been put. But before the king drank of the wine, he made over it the sign of the Cross, and named the Name of God over it. Immediately the cup shivered to atoms in his hand. That is always true of sincere, earnest prayer. Many a cup which is fair without and good to look upon, of which the soul would like to drink, will be found to be full of poison when it is prayed over before it is drunk.

Hear once again that Voice that sounds out of Gethsemane, the Voice of that faithful Bugler, that great Lover of our souls: *Watch ye and pray, lest ye enter into temptation.*

Now unto him that is able to keep you from falling, and to present you faultless before the presence of his glory with exceeding joy, to the only wise God our Saviour, be glory and majesty, dominion and power, both now and ever. Amen.

IX
PRAYER AND YOUR TROUBLE

Call upon me in the day of trouble: I will deliver thee, and thou shalt glorify me (Ps. 50:15)

PRAYER AND YOUR TROUBLE

Call upon me in the day of trouble: I will deliver thee, and thou
shalt glorify me (Ps. 50:15).

How daring God is! What great commitments He makes
to the soul of man! He is the covenant-making and the
covenant-keeping God. As Peter put it, God has given us
exceeding great and precious promises. Here is one of them:
Call upon me in the day of trouble: I will deliver thee.

Defoe, the author of *Robinson Crusoe*, was not only a
great storyteller but a wise Christian. There is a vast
amount of practical, everyday theology packed in the pages
of his marvelous narrative of the shipwreck and island life
of Robinson Crusoe.

Some time after Robinson Crusoe had been cast on the
island, he became desperately ill. It is unpleasant to be sick
at home, where you have friends and members of your family
to care for you, or in the hospital, where you have the help
of doctors and nurses; but it is much worse to be sick on a
lonely island. With great effort Robinson managed to open
the lid of a chest which he had retrieved from the wrecked
ship. Searching for medicine, and divinely led (he was certain of this), he found in the chest not only medicine for his
body but medicine for his soul — a Bible. After he had
taken the medicine, he opened the Bible, and the first words
on which his eye fell were these from Psalm 50:

Call upon me in the day of trouble: I will deliver thee,
and thou shalt glorify me.

This text greatly impressed Robinson Crusoe, and he began to hope that perhaps God would heal him of his sickness, deliver him from his solitary island and bring him back
to his native land and to his friends once more. Before he
went to bed that night he did a thing which he had never

done before in his life: he knelt down and prayed, and in his prayer he asked God that He might fulfill the promise of that verse in his own life, heal him of his sickness and deliver him from his wave-washed island. When he had so prayed, he felt much relieved and sank into an untroubled sleep. Some days afterwards he was walking along the shore with his gun over his shoulder; suddenly his heart almost stopped as he saw on the sand the imprint of the foot of a savage. He fled immediately to his stockade, and, climbing the wall, pulled the ladder in after him. He was filled with terror. Then he recalled those words: *Call upon me in the day of trouble: I will deliver thee,* and he began to lose his fear.

This verse in which the shipwrecked mariner found comfort is of value for all, for trouble comes to all. The verse sets before us the fact of trouble, what we should do and where we should go when trouble comes, and what God promises He will do.

I. THE FACT OF TROUBLE

Trouble is universal. It is no respecter of persons. It comes to a lonely shipwrecked sailor like Robinson Crusoe on his solitary island; it comes to the man who rubs elbows with millions of other men in the great cities of the world. Man is born to trouble as the sparks fly upward. Light a brush fire toward the evening, and watch the sparks as they fly upward! They are the inevitable result and accompaniment of the fire. Likewise, wherever the fire of life is lighted, wherever a man passes through the experiences of this world, the sparks of trouble fly upward. There are all kinds of troubles: troubles of body; troubles of mind; troubles of soul; troubles we bring upon ourselves; troubles others bring upon us. We are troubled by sorrow, fear, loneliness, death and sin — the sorest of all troubles. Ofttimes those who seem to have the fewest troubles, in reality have the most. Like the king on the walls of Samaria, they wear their sackcloth within.

> If every man's internal care
> Were written on his brow,
> How many who our envy share
> Would have our pity now.

Early in the morning the streets and sidewalks of the city begin to resound with the marching feet of the toilers and the buyers and sellers. At noon the sound reaches its loudest volume; then it begins to decrease, until, when midnight comes, the streets are deserted, save for the night watchman and the reveler. But the sound of the marching feet of the army of the troubled never ceases. Morning, noon, evening and midnight I hear them marching by in an endless procession. March! March! March!

II. THE PURPOSE OF TROUBLE

Since trouble is the lot of man in this life, it must have some good and high purpose. It would indeed be a strange world if there were no troubles, no aches, pains, sorrows, tears or anxieties. Life would be a Dead Sea of bliss, in which one could float, but could not swim or make progress. Trouble is the foil against which the highest virtues shine. When I think about heaven, where there will be no trouble, I wonder what is to take the place there of those things which are the greatest in life, and which are related to trouble, for how could there be courage if there were no danger? How could there be tenderness if there were no pain? How could there be sympathy and compassion if there were no hardship? How could there be hope if there were no night of doubt? Yes, there must be some great and good purpose in our troubled lives.

Two men were once discussing the reason why we cannot see the stars in the daytime. The stars are still there; they are not farther away by day than they are by night. Why is it that we cannot see them? One ventured the opinion that if a man went far enough into a hole in the earth and looked up, he could see the stars by day. The other doubted that such would be the case, but agreed to make the experiment. He was lowered in a basket into a well. After he had been lowered for some distance, those who were holding the rope asked him if he could see the stars. He said, "No." Again after he had gone lower, they asked him if he could see the stars. Again his answer was, "No." But when he had been lowered to a great depth, he looked up, and, lo, he could see the stars. God lowers men into the well of trouble that they may see the stars, that they may know the great glories which are hidden from them by the sunlight of prosperity.

At the end of his great book *The Republic*, Plato tells of the dream of the Greek soldier Erus, who had fallen in battle, and, according to his story, was transported into the future world, where he saw the wicked condemned and the righteous rewarded. Plato tells also that after a period of years those who had been sent to the lower regions and punished, and those who came down from heaven to begin life over again, were given an opportunity by Lachesis, the Daughter of Necessity, to choose their lot in a new life. Exceedingly strange choices were made by this multitude of souls. Some of the worst choices, Plato tells us, were made by those who had come down from heaven and had never had the discipline and experience of trouble. Those who came up from the earth and the lower regions were much more careful in their choice. Trouble is one of life's great teachers.

III. WHERE TO GO WHEN TROUBLE COMES

Call upon me in the day of trouble: I will deliver thee. There is nothing ambiguous or uncertain about that. *Call upon me,* God says, and He promises, *I will deliver thee.*

Some men sink and collapse in helplessness and fear when

trouble comes to them. Others rebel against God, and do what Job's wife advised him to do: *Curse God, and die.* Others accept trouble, but with a grim, stoical submission. That is not what God tells us to do. He says, *Call upon me in the day of trouble: I will deliver thee.*

The Bible has little to say about God as an abstraction, and little to say in definition of His attributes. What it does is to present Him and declare Him as the "performing" God, the God who *acts*. Not only that, He is a *covenant-making* God. Here is one of His covenants: *Call upon me in the day of trouble: I will deliver thee.* When men do that, they recognize that God is over all, that there is a Higher Will at work in the world, that no trouble can come to us without God's permission.

There are many persons who can underline this verse with the red ink of personal experience. In the time of their trouble they called on God. Deliverance came, and came in a way that left no doubt in their minds as to whether or not God had heard and answered them. The Bible is full of such instances. When the chariots of Pharaoh were rumbling behind Israel, and the Red Sea yawned before them, Moses called upon God, and God stretched out His arm and opened a way for them through the Red Sea. When Sennacherib, king of Assyria, sent his blasphemous and insulting letter to the king of Judah, Hezekiah took the letter and spread it out before the Lord, and God heard him and smote the Assyrian host.

> The Angel of Death spread his wings on the blast,
> And breathed in the face of the foe as he passed.

The Bible resounds with the prayers of those who were in trouble and found that God was their refuge and strength, a very present help in time of trouble. Hagar, about to perish, cried to God in the wilderness for herself and for her child, and God showed her a fountain of water. Elijah, in his despair, called upon God in the wilderness, and God showed him His glory and revived his faith. Hezekiah, sorely smitten and on the brink of the grave, in great bitterness called upon God, and God sent the shadow back upon the face of the dial and added years to his life. Hannah in her bitterness of soul, prayed in the Holy House at Shiloh, and God heard her prayer and gave her Samuel. Jonah cried to God out of the belly of the great fish, when he went *down to the bottoms of the mountains*, when the depths closed about him and the weeds were wrapped about his head, and God delivered him and gave him another opportunity to do His will and preach repentance unto Nineveh. Jacob, struggling in the darkness with the angel on the ford of the Jabbok, *wept, and made supplication unto him,* and *had power over the angel,* and was changed from Jacob the Supplanter to Israel the Prince of God.

The Syrophoenician woman cried to God for her only daughter, and Christ said, *O woman, great is thy faith: be it unto thee even as thou wilt.* The father of the demoniac boy cried to Jesus when He came down from the Mount of Transfiguration: *If thou canst do any thing, have compassion on us, and help us.* And Jesus healed his son. Paul, in his darkness and blindness, prayed to God in the house of Judas at Damascus, and God heard him and opened his eyes and sent him forth with the light of the truth in his soul to proclaim the everlasting Gospel. Job, overwhelmed with his afflictions and calamities, smitten in body and in soul, sent up a prayer to God, and God heard him and gave him back his property and seven new sons and three new daughters. What is more, He taught him to say, *Though he slay me, yet will I trust in him.* David, out of the darkness of his transgression and sin, called upon God: *Have mercy upon me, O Lord, according to thy lovingkindness: according to the multitude of thy tender mercies, blot out my transgressions;* God heard him and forgave his sin; and through his repentance and forgiveness David still teaches transgressors the ways of God. These cried out of the depths — *Out of the depths have I cried unto thee* — and God answered and His deliverance gives us great encouragement in our prayers. Seeing that we have a great High Priest who is touched with the feeling of our infirmities, *let us therefore come boldly unto the throne of grace, that we may obtain mercy, and find grace to help in time of need.* What would we do without prayer?

> From ev'ry stormy wind that blows,
> From ev'ry swelling tide of woes,
> There is a calm, a sure retreat,
> 'Tis found beneath the mercy seat.
>
> Ah, whither could we flee for aid,
> When tempted, desolate, dismayed,
> Or how the hosts of hell defeat,
> Had suffering saints no mercy seat?

IV. THE HIGHER DELIVERANCE

But what of those who were not delivered when they prayed? As clearly as I saw it then so many years ago, I can see it now. A young minister, just beginning my work, I stepped to the window of a shabby ticket office of the Erie Railroad in New York to buy a ticket. The man saw the minister's order, and when he made out the ticket, he asked, "Do you believe in prayer?" Then he told me of the long illness of his wife, and how eagerly, but unavailingly, they had prayed for her recovery. I gave him the best answer I knew. What shall we say, then, about those who in their trouble called upon God, who had marked this verse in their Bibles, had trusted in this promise, but one day prayed and were not delivered?

A British mother who had a son in the army in France during the first World War, went daily to special services and masses (she was a Roman Catholic) and begged God to watch over her son and bring him safely back from the war. One morning as she returned from mass, she found at her home a telegram from the War Department, telling her of the death of her son who had been killed in battle. She said to her friends, "I am through with religion. Either there is no God, or He doesn't care."

What shall we say, then, about such cases? The answer is this: God has more than one kind of deliverance. As Robinson Crusoe mused over this verse, he began to think less about deliverance from his solitary island and more about his relationship to God. He began to put the emphasis upon the third clause of this great verse: *Thou shalt glorify me.*

There is a higher deliverance than mere deliverance from the thing that troubles us or grieves us. There is a deliverance that brings us into fellowship with God. There is a deliverance that permits us to see that, when we are exercised thereby, when we see God's hand in our trouble — for no trouble comes without His permission — however grievous it may be at present, afterwards it will *yield the peaceable fruit of righteousness*; and so we shall glorify the Name of God.

Friends of mine were given by God a little child, a lovely daughter. She was the joy of their home and the apple of their eye. But one day the child was taken sick. These earnest Christians called upon God to deliver, but the life of the child was not spared. Yet this providence did not destroy their faith, but deepened it. The father said that he attributed his deeper experience as a Christian to that sorrow, and he testified that it brought him the faith, never to be shaken, that God always answers prayer and always delivers, although His deliverance may be above that for which we ask. Such an incident as this throws light upon that great expression of the apostle, namely, that God is able to do for us *exceeding abundantly above all that we ask or think*. Yes, all-wise and tender Heavenly Father, how true that is!

Never hesitate, then, to call upon God. Never doubt that

He hears. Never doubt that in His own way He will deliver. If we call upon Him, He will always do far above what we can ask or think.

The most grievous of all troubles is sin. Sin is the fountain and source of all other troubles. It is regarding this trouble, above all others, that the great promises of God's deliverances are made. When Robinson Crusoe first read that verse, *Call upon me in the day of trouble: I will deliver thee,* he was thinking only of deliverance from his lonely life on the wave-swept island. But afterwards, as he read the Bible, he began to think not about his physical and geographical condition, but about his spiritual condition; not how far he was from England and his fellowmen, but how far he was from God. He began to pray to God to deliver him, and he discovered that deliverance from sin is a much greater blessing than deliverance from affliction.

Only God can work the great miracle of deliverance from sin. Only God can speak peace to the troubled conscience. *Being justified by faith, we have peace with God through our Lord Jesus Christ.* Thousands upon thousands of souls, since the days of Paul, who wrote those words, down to the present day, have found this verse to be true. The searchlight of His love from the Cross shone through the darkness and the gloom of their lives and lighted the way as their penitent souls went home to God.

Call upon me in the day of trouble: I will deliver thee, and thou shalt glorify me. That is the great purpose of life, and is the great possibility of life: that by our repentance, faith and trust in God amid all our troubles and trials, our transgressions and failures, we should glorify God. Reader, you have that sublime capacity! No matter what your life has been, no matter what it is today, no matter how dark your horizon may seem to you, you can glorify God! God can make, as He says He will, your Valley of Achor, your Valley of Trouble, a place of hope and of glory.